Manifesting Your Dreams
JOURNAL

BONNIE BARNESS

MANIFESTING YOUR DREAMS JOURNAL

Copyright ©2017 by Bonnie Barness. All rights reserved.

Table of Contents

A NOTE FROM THE AUTHOR 6

THE MAGICAL PLACE OF AWARENESS 9

20 GIFTS FOR YOUR JOURNEY 39

NINE MANIFESTING CHARMS 43

THE MANIFESTING OASIS 99

LIVING IN PASSION 103

ABOUT THE AUTHOR 107

A Note from the Author

Dear Authentic You!

You are about to embark on an amazing manifesting adventure. As you move forward on your new path, you will go to a higher level of conscious awareness and receive the *Manifesting Principals and Charms* that will support you in creating your chosen dream.

You have already taken the first step onto your new path. You did this at the moment you connected with the deep and powerful desire within your True Authentic Self to experience more excitement and fulfillment in your life.

You have the ability to create, through your own thoughts and actions, much of what you desire. Today is truly the first day of the rest of your life and you have chosen to use it to begin manifesting your next dream.

Know that I am here by your side in this adventure of passion and connection to your True Self. Now is the time. This is the moment to create the Authentic Life that reflects the unique and amazing YOU in the world. Are you ready to *Experience the Shift*?

Enjoy Manifesting!

Manifesting
On Your New Path

Congratulations!

You have now stepped onto your new path, one filled with adventures and powerful experiences. With each step you take, you will gain *Gifts* that will support you in living a life connected with your True Authentic Self.

This path will lead you to a new way of thinking and being in the world. A SHIFT will begin to occur. Connected with your strong desire and wish to have more in your life, you have taken the first step. To take your second step, make the decision, right now, to do whatever it takes to create a truly Authentic Life that reflects your True Self in the world.

1. Do you want more passion and fulfillment in your life?

2. Have you made the decision to do whatever it takes to create it?

For those of you who have already been traveling on your new path since going through the *Creating Your Authentic Path Weekend Workshop* or after reading the *Experiencing the Shift Journal* and Book, please ask yourself these questions, as well. Get ready to enjoy the new, exciting experiences you will have as you continue moving forward towards *Manifesting Your Dreams*.

Now that you have taken your first exciting steps onto your new path, you are ready to take the next one, entering into the Magical Place of Awareness. It is here that you will gain the *Knowledge and Manifesting Principals* that will allow you to create your dreams. As you take this next step on your new path, you will attain another level of awareness. This higher vantage point will allow you to observe new, previously unseen, options and possibilities. This wider lens will provide you with the means to live your life filled with passion and a deep sense of fulfillment.

Are you ready to take the next step towards Manifesting Your Dreams?

The Magical Place of Awareness

CAVE ONE: YOUR *True Self*

1. You, your True Self, is unique and wonderful. Your True Self has a voice, your True Voice. All words spoken by your True Voice are kind, compassionate, wise and supportive. As you listen closely, you can hear what your True Voice is saying about your ability to *Manifest Your Dreams*. In the first space on each line, write the words that your True Voice is saying to you.

    _____ _____
    _____ _____
    _____ _____
    _____ _____

2. Say, aloud, the first word that you have written down above.

3. Notice the feeling that follows.

4. Describe your feeling next to the word.

5. Continue this process for each word, spoken by your True Voice, on your list.

6. Describe what your True Self *Manifesting Your Dreams* looks like. Draw a picture if you choose.

CAVE TWO: YOUR *False Self*

1. Your False Self, who you believe you are at times, has a voice, your False Voice. All words spoken by your False Voice are negative, critical and judgmental. If your thoughts are positive and your feelings are hopeful about the new adventure ahead, you are connected to your True Self and your True Voice. If you thoughts and feelings are filled with judgment, you are connected to your False Self and False Voice. In the first space on each line, please write down the words that your False Voice is saying when you think about embarking on your new manifesting adventure

_____   _____

_____   _____

_____   _____

_____   _____

2. Say, aloud, the first word that you have written above.

3. Notice the feeling that follows.

4. Describe your feelings next to the word.

5. Continue the process for each word, spoken by your False Voice, on your list.

6. Describe what your False Self looks like. Draw a picture if you choose.

THE COPPER Scale

1. Our feelings flow from our thoughts and affect the choices we make. The choices we make create, for the most part, the life that we have. *Manifesting Your Dreams*, and enjoying the process along the way, happens when you are connected to your True Self. Think of a time, in the past, when you reached a desired goal. Write in the space below the thoughts and feelings you had throughout the entire process—from the first original idea to the *Actualization of Your Dream*.

Thoughts

Feelings

2. Now, think of a time when you went after something and it did not come to fruition. Write below the thoughts and feelings you had throughout the entire process.

Thoughts

Feelings

The knowledge, found here in the Magical Place of Awareness, is the basis of your SHIFT in perspective that will allow you to create a life filled with inner peace and joy. A deeper understanding of the *SHIFT Principals* can be gained in the *Experiencing the Shift Journal* and Book.

You are about to receive additional knowledge and insights that will support you in manifesting a wonderful and fulfilling life. *Manifesting* is the same as goal-setting and reaching a desired outcome yet it can also feel completely different. Achieving a goal often feels like hard work. It may involve struggle and sacrifice. In the past, obstacles may have prevented you from reaching the goals that you desired the most.

Manifesting can be a very different experience. It is one filled with joy, gratitude and inspiration. Resistance and barriers can seem to dissolve almost effortlessly. What may have felt difficult in the past, now, is easy and fun. Utilizing the *Manifesting Principals*, here and now, will allow you to move forward towards your dream with a different level of consciousness and in a unique and new way.

You are about to receive the *Manifesting Principals*, the foundation for manifesting your chosen dream, which will add to the new awareness you have already gained. Are you ready to move to a higher level of consciousness and take the next step on your new path?

THE FOREST: *Parallel Realities*

1. At this moment, different *Parallel Realities* exist. In each moment, you have the ability to choose from an infinite amount of possibilities. How will you will *BE* in the world? What will you *DO*? Each of these choices, moment to moment, begins to manifest an outcome, a *Parallel Reality* from the one you are in right now.

   Take some time to think about an opportunity available to you earlier today, last week, or at a significant moment in your life and observe the choice you made. Write below other options that were available to you at the time.

   OPPORTUNITY/SITUATION

   FOUR OPTIONS AVAILABLE

   1.
   2.
   3.
   4.

   OPTION YOU CHOSE

2. Now, write below the three options available that you did not take and what would likely have occurred had you chosen each one.

   Option 1

   Option 2

   Option 3

   Please describe what actually occurred.

   Over the next days and weeks, take some time and go through this process for other choices that you have made. Indicate below what you discover.

CLEARING IN THE WOODS:
Be Do Have

1. The process of *Manifesting Your Dream* begins with your connection to your True Authentic Self which is the source of all your creativity and power. In order to have whatever it is that you wish to manifest, you must first *BE*. Close your eyes and get in touch with your True Self. Think of a time when you felt great during or after having achieved a goal. Choose a moment in your life when you felt you could do anything, create anything. Now open your eyes, and describe below how you felt to *BE*.

2. Once you are connected with your inner power and the source of your creativity, it is necessary to take action, to *DO*, in order to manifest. Think of a time when you accomplished a goal you had set for yourself. Now describe the actions that you took to reach the desired outcome.

3. Once you have connected with your inner source of creativity and then taken the action necessary, you will be on your way to *HAVE* that which you wish to manifest. Think back on a time when you connected with your desire and your True Self, took specific actions and achieved what you desired. Now describe it below.

THE AMPHITHEATER:
Manifesting Vibration

1. You are made of energy. Energy vibrates at different frequencies. When you vibrate at a higher frequency, you feel wonderful, when you vibrate at a lower frequency, you don't feel as good.

   Pay attention to how you are feeling over the next few days and notice the differences in your energy, your vibration. On the lines below, describe what you notice.

Energy (High, Medium, Low)	Associated Feeling

2 Everything and everyone is made up of the same energy, all vibrating at different frequencies. Pay attention to the people around you and notice how you feel when you are with them. In the space below, write down each person's name, what you notice about their energy and how you feel in each person's presence.

Person   *Energy/Vibration*   *Your Feeling*

3. Now, notice the *Energetic Vibrations* and how you feel when you are in different environments including your home, nature, and the workplace.

Place   *Energy/Vibration*   *Your Feeling*

4. Notice the level of your energy, the frequency of your *Energetic Vibration*. How do you feeling when you are sitting, walking, dancing and during times of rest and activity?

Activity	Energy/Vibration	Your Feeling

Being aware of *Energetic Vibrations* will allow you to connect with your own *Manifesting Vibrations*. Can you feel the excitement growing within? Get ready! You are about to start on your *Manifesting Path!*

THE GLASS CHALET: ASPECTS OF *Your Mind*

1. Thoughts, for the most part, create your life. Thus, understanding your thoughts is essential to *Manifesting Your Dreams*. When you hear your thoughts, you are connected to your conscious mind. If you take time to listen, you can become aware of all of your conscious thoughts. List some thoughts you are having right now.

Thoughts

2. Many of our actions and thoughts take place without our being aware of either. We are unconscious of them. Sometimes, people we are close to can point out something that we have been previously unaware. List some of your behaviors that you were unaware of until they were brought to your attention.

3. You remember some of your past experiences. Others you do not. Yet, your subconscious mind holds them all. Many of these experiences influence you and your choices today. When they are in your subconscious and you have not accessed them, they can create resistance to what your conscious mind wants to manifest. Have you ever become aware of any past experiences that had previously been unconscious? If you have, please list them below.

4. Your body, also, holds onto emotions from past experiences. These emotions, though you are unaware of them, also can have a strong influence on your life. In order to remove the blocks that impact your ability to create what you desire, you must reach into your subconscious. This takes courage and strength. Are you open to exploring your subconscious? What feelings, thoughts, and bodily sensations come up for you when you consider journeying into this hidden place within?

5. When we use our imagination and connect it to our emotions and other senses, our mind recognizes it as real. Close your eyes now and imagine yourself in a beautiful relaxing place. Feel it. See it. Then open your eyes and describe the experience below.

THE ASHRAM: YOUR PRECIOUS *Manifesting Tools*

1. We all have *Precious Energy* to create what we desire in our life. It is Precious because it's ours and it is finite. We have the ability to choose how we use our *Precious Energy*. Take a moment now to think about and then describe specifically how you are using your *Precious Energy*.

2. With whom do you expend your *Precious Energy* and how?

3. We all have *Precious Time* available to create our Authentic Life, a life of passion. In the world we live in, there is a finite amount of time each day. You have the ability to choose how you will use this very *Precious Manifesting Tool*. Please describe how you are using your *Precious Time* right now.

4. How and with whom do you share some of your *Precious Time*?

5. We all have various resources including money available to create our Authentic Life. Right now, you have a certain amount of money and resources available to you. It is Precious because it is yours. For the most part, you have the ability to determine how you will use this *Manifesting Tool*. Please describe how you are using your *Precious Resources* right now.

6. With whom do you share some of your *Precious Resources* and how?

THE LAUREL TREE: TRAVELING *Through Time*

1. In your mind, you are able to go back in time. You can also imagine yourself in some future time. When you immerse yourself in each of these internal experiences, it becomes imprinted into your being just as experiences that you have when interacting in the physical world. Think back to a time when you felt happy and excited. Now close your eyes and allow yourself to go back in time in your mind's eye. In the space below, describe, in detail, what you see, sense and feel.

2. Now, think about yourself in the future doing something that you enjoy. Go through the same process as above and write what you experience.

THE NIGHT'S SKY: PARTNERING
With the Universe

1. When our dreams are in alignment with our destiny, manifesting is a strong potential reality. Think of something that you manifested in your life that you knew was meant to be and describe it below.

   _____
   _____
   _____
   _____

2. When our dreams are in alignment with our destiny, we often notice synchronicity and coincidences that support the process of manifesting. Think of a time when you felt that you were truly *Partnering with the Universe*. Describe it below.

THE STREAM: BEING IN *the Flow*

1. When you are *In the Flow*, you can feel it. Everything feels effortless and easy. Think of a time when you were *In the Flow*. Where were you?

2. What were you doing?

3. How did you feel?

4. When you are *In the Flow* and an obstacle comes across your path, you are able to deal with it effectively while keeping your focus on your destination. Think back to a time when you were *In the Flow* and an obstacle came into your path. Where were you?

5. What was the obstacle?

6. How did you deal with obstacle?

7. What did you do to stay focused on your destination?

THE BOULDER: LIVING IN *the Now*

1. Time and space are part of our physical reality. When we view life from a different perspective, we can see that all we have is THIS moment. THIS moment. THIS moment. Each moment is precious. Please write your thoughts and reflections on this concept.

2. Often, in our society, we are focused on the past or the future and miss out on *Living in the NOW*. It is important to learn and heal from the past and to look into the future in order to create a beautiful life for ourselves. Balance is the key. As you move forward on your *Manifesting Path*, the knowledge that all you have is *NOW* will enhance and transform your journey. Reflect on the way you have gone through life until this very moment. What do you see? What changes can you make to appreciate each moment and to live more fully in the *NOW*?

3. Even when we *Travel Through Time*, all we have is each moment, each experience in the *NOW*. Going through life with this heightened awareness allows us to value our life and ourselves each and every moment. Consider how living life with this new awareness could transform your conscious experience of life.

Thoughts

JIMINY Cricket

Jiminy sits on your shoulder and speaks into your ear as you move forward on your new path. Jiminy helps you stay aware of the knowledge gained throughout your journey. With this awareness always present, you have a greater ability to make choices that can support your dreams becoming a reality. You may have met Jiminy here in the Magical Place of Awareness already! Listening to Jiminy allows you to be consciously involved in creating the life that you desire as you move forward on your new path and SHIFT into a new level of conscious awareness.

1. Would you like your companion to have a different name? If you would, what will you choose?

2. Does your companion have a form? If so, describe or draw what you see or imagine.

3. As you begin to *Experience the Shift*, new insights will occur. Due to these realizations, often, you will choose to replace old thoughts and behaviors with new ones that reflect your True Self in the world. As you move forward on your exciting journey, indicate the new insights received and the words you hear Jiminy speak.

New Insights	Words Spoken
★	
★	
★	
★	
★	
★	
★	
★	
★	
★	
★	
★	

4. If you have been traveling on your new path for awhile and are *Experiencing the Shift,* please indicate what new insights you have had so far. Then, indicate what Jiminy says to you each day that supports your new way of being in the world.

New Insights *Words Spoken*

★ _____ _____

★ _____ _____

★ _____ _____

★ _____ _____

★ _____ _____

★ _____ _____

★ _____ _____

★ _____ _____

★ _____ _____

★ _____ _____

★ _____ _____

★ _____ _____

My Reflections

20 Gifts For Your *Journey*

YOUR 20 Gifts

In the, *Experiencing the Shift Journal* and Book, you received the 20 Gifts for Creating Your Authentic Path. As you move forward on your new path, choose the specific gifts that will make your dream come true!

GIFT ONE: Trust Your Perspective

GIFT TWO: Do Something For Yourself Every Day

GIFT THREE: Put Your Well-Being As Your Priority

GIFT FOUR: Honor Yourself

GIFT FIVE: Stop Unwanted Thoughts

GIFT SIX: Create Your World Within The World-at-Large

GIFT SEVEN: Take an Honest Look

GIFT EIGHT: Choose Your Thoughts, Beliefs, and Values

GIFT NINE: Treat Others with Respect, Appreciation, and Kindness

GIFT TEN: Strengthen Your Detachment Muscle

GIFT ELEVEN: Check Out Your Assumptions

GIFT TWELVE: Look At The Whole Picture

GIFT THIRTEEN: Open Your Eyes To The Present Reality

GIFT FOURTEEN: Use Your Emotional Intelligence

GIFT FIFTEEN: Prepare For Your Personal Marathon

GIFT SIXTEEN: Healthy Boundaries

GIFT SEVENTEEN: Choose Intimacy

GIFT EIGHTEEN: Discover Your Passions

GIFT NINETEEN: Sustain Focus To Create

GIFT TWENTY: Gratitude

Nine Manifesting *Charms*

CHARM ONE: CHOOSE FROM
Infinite Possibilities

As you move forward on your exciting life's journey, you will be receiving a variety of *Charms* to use for manifesting. When you use your *Charms* together with the specific *Gifts* that are on your new path, you can Actualize your True Self in the World.

1. Utilize your new awareness about *Parallel Realities* and write down different realities, dreams, that you may be interested in manifesting. *Discover Your Passions*, Gift 18, consider what you are passionate about and would love to connect with at this moment in time.

2. In considering which one you wish to manifest, please ask the following questions:

   ★ Why do I wish to manifest this dream?

   ★ Is it my dream or someone else's dream?

   ★ Is my desire coming from my True Voice or my False Voice?

   ★ Am I *Trusting My Perspective*, Gift 1, choosing to go after what I want to create?

   ★ When actualized, will this dream reflect my True Self in the world?

3. Now, choose the dream you wish to manifest in your life!

CHARM TWO: VISUALIZE
Your Dream Manifested

1. When you imagine your life with your dream already manifested, you are going into a *Parallel Reality*. Using your new awareness about your ability to *Travel Through Time*, see yourself in the future living the dream you are about to begin manifesting right now. Please describe in as much detail as possible what you see. What do you look like? Where are you? What are you wearing? What do you pick up with your various senses?

2. Close your eyes and allow yourself to feel the joy and happiness within as you *BE DO* and *HAVE* your dream. Feel your energy SHIFT to the manifesting level of high vibration as you imagine that it is actually taking place right now, that you are there experiencing it at this very moment. Now open your eyes and describe what you are feeling.

3. Feel how much you want this to become your reality. Can you put it into words?

4. Now write a letter, from the Future You to your True Authentic Self right here and now. In the letter, describe the life you are living, Your Dream Manifested.

Dear Authentic ME!

CHARM THREE: DESIGN YOUR MANIFESTING *Dream Map*

1. Spend some time researching what it will take to *Manifest Your Dream*. Then, write down what you learned.

   ★

   ★

   ★

   ★

   ★

   ★

   ★

   ★

   ★

2. Determine the amount of *Precious Manifesting Energy, Time and Resources* that are needed to *Manifest Your Dream*.

Precious Energy *Precious Time* *Precious Resources*

3. Using Gift 7, *Take an Honest Look* at the amount of *Precious Manifesting Energy, Time and Resources* you have available to *Manifest Your Dream*. Then, ask yourself, the following questions:

★ Do I want to *Manifest My Dream* now or possibly later? Why?

★ Based on the amount of *Precious Manifesting Energy, Time and Resources* available at this time in my life would I like to manifest a different dream? Why? Why not?

★ Is *Living in Balance* and *Putting My Well-Being, as a Priority,* Gift 3, important for me while I *Manifest My Dream*? Why? Why not?

4. Now, reflect on the new options and possibilities that will follow once your dream has been manifested. Describe what you discover.

5. Choose and describe the dream you wish to manifest starting right now.

6. Now that you have chosen the dream you wish to manifest, it is time to create your own *Manifesting Dream Map* to make your dream a reality. Here are some questions to ask yourself that can be helpful in creating your special *Manifesting Dream Map*.

★ Am I willing to do whatever it takes, that is a reflection of my True Self, to *Manifest My Dream*?

★ How much of my *Precious Energy, Time and Resources* will I be putting into *Manifesting My Dream*?

Precious Energy:

Precious Time:

Precious Money:

Other Precious Resources:

★ Am I willing to *Do Something for Myself Each Day*, Gift 2, connecting to the power I have within, as I *Manifest My Dream*?

★ What knowledge about myself, other people and life have I gained that will support my manifesting efforts, and which will I incorporate into my *Manifesting Dream Map*?

★ What actions did I take in the past that supported achieving previous goals? Which would I like to incorporate in my *Manifesting Dream Map*?

My Manifesting Dream Map

MANIFESTING ACTIONS TO MY DREAM

★ Manifesting Action 1
★ Manifesting Action 2
★ Manifesting Action 3
★ Manifesting Action 4
★ Manifesting Action 5
★ Manifesting Action 6
★ Manifesting Action 7
★ Manifesting Action 8
★ Manifesting Action 9
★ Manifesting Action 10
★ Manifesting Action 11
★ Manifesting Action 12

Actualization of My True Self in the World!

CHARM FOUR: SHIFT WITH YOUR *Manifesting Team*

1. Now that you are listening to your True Voice and connecting more and more with your True Self, you are feeling the joy and power within yourself grow. You are beginning to *Experience the Shift* in perspective, seeing and thinking in a new way.

    You are ready to move further along on your *Manifesting Path*. As you do so, you may find that it may benefit you to have a special team of people who can provide you with the emotional, psychological, and physical support needed as you walk forward utilizing your *Manifesting Dream Map*. They may be friends, family, and/or professional with different expertise.

    Reflect on what type of support would be most beneficial as you start out on your *Manifesting Path*. Write each one below.

    ★

    ★

    ★

    ★

    ★

2. Now that you have identified the type of support that will give you what you need as you begin on your *Manifesting Path*, think of who will provide this need to you. The basic requirement for each team member is that he or she is kind, supportive, and excited for you and what you are doing. Anyone who is in the least bit critical or judgmental should not be on your Manifesting Team. Choose people who will give their full energy to you, during your time together, while enjoying and supporting your amazing journey. *Check Out Your Assumptions*, Gift 11, getting additional information in determining who will be perfect for you in your manifesting adventure.

   If there are people that you know right now, please write down their names. After doing so, reach out to your new *Manifesting Team Members* and bring them into your exciting new adventure.

   ★ _____

   ★ _____

   ★ _____

   ★ _____

3. If there are members of your *Manifesting Team* that you need to find, you can do so in the next days ahead. When you bring them onto the team, write down their names above. Congratulations! You are on your way to Actualizing Your Dream, taking it from your mind's eye into the physical reality.

   Remember to utilize Gifts 16, *Healthy Boundaries* and 17, *Choose Intimacy* when selecting your *Manifesting Team Members*. Know that you get to determine, using your Gift 6, *Creating Your World Within the World*, who is going to be in your *World-at-Large*.

4. You may also choose to have a group become a part of your *Manifesting Dream Team*. You can take a fun and inspiring class, become a part of a social or networking group, or attend a support program. If you would like to add a group to your *Manifesting Dream Team*, please write down the name, place and time that your group meets.

Name	Place	Time
★		
★		
★		
★		
★		
★		
★		
★		
★		

CHARM FIVE: TAKE YOUR FIRST *Manifesting Action*

Congratulations! You have created a pathway to your dream and have your *Manifesting Team* in place. Are there any actions that you will need to take in preparation for the first action of your manifesting plan? If there is, please write them here and then take them!

★

Are you ready to Manifest Your Dream? Get ready! What is your first manifesting action?

1. Visualize the first action that will begin your manifesting process. See it! Feel it! BE it!

2. Connect with your intensely wonderful desire to *Manifest Your Dream. Honor Yourself*, Gift 4. Feel how much you want it. Connect with your True Self and listen to your True Voice. Allow yourself to feel the desire flow throughout your entire being and then give yourself what you need. Believe in yourself and take your first action in manifesting your dream - right now!

3. How wonderful! You just took the first step in manifesting your Future Self in the world. How does it feel? Describe below your inner and outer experience.

4. Are you ready to take the next manifesting action? If you are, use this charm again. BE and then DO. You are on your way! Are you ready to take it? Get Ready. Get set. Go!!!!

CHARM SIX: MOVE THROUGH *Manifesting Barriers*

1. As you, move forward on your *Manifesting Path*, taking the next actions chosen to *Manifest Your Dream*, some resistance or barriers may arise. Here are some potential ones that may cross your Path.

   ★ Your False Voice

   ★ Other People's Opinions

   ★ Old Beliefs

   ★ Your Subconscious Mind

If your feel resistance to moving forward, take some time and identify WHERE the resistance is coming from and write it below.

2. In order to move through the resistance, it is first important to identify WHAT it is. To start this process, you must first *Honor Yourself*, Gift 4, and listen to your True Voice. What do you hear? If you are conscious of what the resistance is, describe the thoughts and beliefs that are coming up. Also, identify anything external that may be related to the block or obstacle. This action will help you move through the potential obstacle.

Internal

External

3. When you *Honor Yourself*, Gift 4, you *Allow Yourself to Feel*. Next, please identify the emotions that you are feeling and any discomfort you may be having in your body in relationship to the resistance.

Emotions

Physical Discomfort

4. As you look at your *Manifesting Dream Map*, you may feel overwhelmed. It is important to stop and look within to hear the thoughts that you are having. Often, we feel overwhelmed because there seems to be SO much to do. A lot of fear may arise. Please write down below any thoughts and feelings you may be having.

_____

_____

_____

_____

5. Your *Manifesting Dream Map* is a step-by-step general guide. *Living in Balance,* as you discovered in *Finding the Balance, A Guide to Sane Living*, is an integral part. *Staying in Balance* during the manifesting process is one of the keys to creating your new reality. Living in the moment by taking one Manifesting Action and not looking at those up ahead will help you to stay connected to your True Self and to *Stay in Balance*.

Change can bring up fear and the feeling of losing control. Being in the moment, living in the *NOW*, allows you to feel in control as you move into your new reality. Connect with the balance you have within yourself right now and write or draw how it feels in the space below.

6. Feelings of fear, guilt, and anger can create blocks to manifesting. These feelings often are related to past experiences. Are you feeling any of these emotions? If you are, describe the emotion and anything that comes up for you that may be related to it.

Feeling

Feeling

Feeling

7. Now, think back to past experiences that may have some connection with what you are now in the process of manifesting. Please write those that were positive. Indicate the thoughts and emotions that come up for you as you do.

8. Next, think back to times when you set a goal and you felt feelings of disappointment, anger, sadness, and/or guilt. Please describe the circumstances and the thoughts and feelings that you had at the time.

Circumstances	*Thoughts*	*Feelings*

9. In the past, when you pursued a goal, did you accept someone else's criticism or judgment as truth? Did you judge yourself and accept this as truth? Write down what you discover when you reflect on these questions.

10. Next, describe any words and/or beliefs of others that may be creating an obstacle, working in opposition to your creative process, as you move forward with your *Manifesting Dream Map*.

Specific Person _____
Words/Beliefs _____

Specific Person _____
Words/Beliefs _____

Specific Person _____
Words/Beliefs _____

Specific Person _____
Words/Beliefs _____

11. Please write in the first column below, any beliefs about yourself and life that are creating an obstacle to your moving forward on your *Manifesting Path*.

_____   _____   _____

_____   _____   _____

_____   _____   _____

12. In the second column, please indicate where and when belief was created.

13. You have the ability to *Choose Your Thoughts, Beliefs, and Values*, Gift 8. First. listen, to your True Voice as it speaks the truth and, in the third column, write the words that you hear. Utilize thfirst Gift that you received on your new path and *Trust Your Perspective*. Next, replace your false belief with this one that is true for you and that will support your dream becoming a reality.

14. Notice the positive strong *Energetic Vibrations* that is flowing as you reconnect with the power within to create and *Manifest Your Dream* and your wonderful life. Write, or draw an image of, how it feels as you *Take Your Power Back* connected now with your True Authentic Self.

NINE MANIFESTING *Charms*   63

15. Recognize that you were living in one reality created by the thoughts, beliefs, feelings and behaviors you had in the past. Realize that you have now chosen to move to a new *Parallel Reality*. In this new reality, you are connected to your True Self, listening to your True Voice and are taking the actions that reflect who you truly are in the world. Write or draw how it feels to be free to be YOU!

16. The power to move through the resistance comes from keeping connected to your True Self, your True Voice. It is about *Keeping Your Power*. Are you giving your power away, right now, to someone else? If you are, please identify the person and what is occurring at this time.

17. If you are giving your power away to another person to interfere with *Manifesting Your Dream*, it is now time to *Take Back Your Power*. To do so, simply listen to your True Voice and use the *Gifts* to connect with your True Self. Below, describe the process that you will follow.

18. When you *Honor Yourself*, Gift 4, you give yourself what you need. After reflection, please indicate what you need in order to move through the resistance and forward on your *Manifesting Path*. You may consider actions that you took in the past, internally and externally that supported your past efforts.

19. Often our False Voice becomes louder as we move forward in manifesting. We can be very hard on ourselves. Our False Voice will have unrealistic expectations, reminding us of what we did not do in the past or what we are not doing right now. If this is your experience, it can create a major block to moving forward on your *Manifesting Path*. Please describe below what you can hear coming from your False Voice.

20. We all do the best we can with the knowledge that we have. Know that you did the best you could in the past, with the knowledge you had at the time. With your new level of awareness and the *Gifts and Charms* you are receiving on this new wonderful path, you have the ability to stay connected to your True Self and to Actualize more of Your True Self in the World than ever before.

    Think about past situations, and *Use Your Emotional Intelligence*, Gift 14, to gain a greater understanding of yourself. Take the knowledge gained to support you in *Manifesting Your Dream*. Describe what you have discovered below. Know that today. is the first day of the rest of your life. The choices you make today will, for the most part, create the life that you will have. Choose wisely.

    Experience   *Knowledge Gained*

21. If you come across a block, a rock in your *Stream of Life*, take a close look at it. Great knowledge is gained through this process. Write down below, what is transpiring.

22. Now, listen to your thoughts. Is your False Voice speaking? If it is, what is it saying? Please write this down in the first column. Then, in the second column, listen to the words of truth, regarding the situation, spoken by your True Voice.

23. Sometimes, we realize that our False Voice is speaking and we want it to stop. If the thoughts continue, we can use specific techniques to *Stop Unwanted Thoughts,* Gift 5. Write down some techniques that you will use.

★ _____

★ _____

★ _____

★ _____

24. Now, look at the *Gifts* and knowledge gained on you new path, and discover what action you will take to *Stay in the Flow* that will support your manifesting process.

Gift   *Action*

CHARM SEVEN: CREATE A NEW *Way of Being*

1. Your life was created, to a large degree, from the choices that you made in the past. The choices and actions that you take now, for the most part, will create your future. Take some time to identify and describe below the specific actions and behaviors, you can do in the days and weeks ahead that will move you forward on your *Manifesting Path*. Consider those that have supported your efforts in the past as well as new ones.

2. One of the greatest feelings comes from *Actualizing Your True Self in the World*. We feel our worst when our actions do not reflect our True Self. Identify which actions and behaviors, you will now eliminate, since they no longer serve you. Please write each one down in the first column.

Behavior   *Need*

3. Understanding yourself is a key to manifesting that which you desire. Each action and behavior listed above filled a need for you. In the second column above, describe the need that each filled and/or still fills.

4. Indicate below, any daily or weekly routines that are associated with these actions and behaviors.

★

5. Now, identify new actions and behaviors that you will bring into your life. Make sure to *Honor Yourself*, Gift 4, by considering your physical, intellectual, emotional, psychological, spiritual and creative needs.

6. Draw a star next to the one(s) that possibly will fill the same needs as the behavior that no longer serves you and will support the *Manifestation of Your Dream*.

7. In *Manifesting Your Dream*, it is important to *Open your Eyes to the Present Reality,* Gift 13. Different emotions will arise as you move forward on your *Manifesting Dream Map*. As they do, please write them below along with the thoughts that accompany them.

Emotions   *Thoughts*

8. When these emotions come up, it is important to *Honor Yourself*, Gift 4, and *Allow Yourself to Feel* each one and then *Give Yourself What You Need*. Please write how you used to repress them and what you will do now when they come up.

Before   *Now*

9. Fear may be an emotion that comes up for you as life begins to reflect your new reality. You may be afraid that you will not be able to realize your dream. It is natural to feel fear. *Allow Yourself to Feel*. Then use Gift 12 and *Look At The Whole Picture*. Look at what you have already manifested. Connect with your True Voice and continue moving forward on your *Manifesting Path*. Listen to your True Voice as it supports you in *Manifesting Your Dream* and reminds you of all that you have already actualized. Write down below, the words that you are hearing

False Voice   *True Voice*

10. Now that you have identified what you need and how to give it to yourself, think about how you will actualize these needs in the world. Then, in the space below, create a schedule that will incorporate these new routines and behaviors in your life.

Monday

Tuesday

Wednesday

Thursday

Friday

Saturday

Sunday

11. *Take an Honest Look*, using your 6th Gift, at the schedule you created and discover if you have considered the *Precious Manifesting Tools* you have available to make sure that it is realistic, sustainable and exciting! Take time now to adjust the schedule based on, Gift 3, *Putting Your Well-Being as Your Priority.*

12. Next utilize what you have learned from looking at previous goals you have set for yourself and from your first manifesting actions and make adjustments in your schedule above and your *Manifesting Dream Map* to support the manifestation of your present dream. Utilize Gift 3 and *Put Your Well-Being as Your Priority* as you write them below.

13. When you *Honor Yourself*, using your 4th Gift, you connect with your inner power to create and manifest. You take back control over your life. Having released the resistance that was holding you back, you are now able to be the *Captain of Your Ship. In the Flow,* you are connected to the unlimited love and abundance within yourself and all around. As you move forward on your *Manifesting Path*, *Honor Yourself*, felt this power and write down how it feels to have your hands on the wheel of your beautiful *Ship*.

CHARM EIGHT: STAY *in the Flow*

1. When you are *In the Flow*, your experience during the manifesting process is fun and exciting. There is an ease to the process that is unlike the past when you worked towards a goal.

   When you are *In the Flow*, it is like a stream that you are at one with, flowing together towards your manifesting destination. You may come upon rocks but just as the stream effortlessly and easily flows around them, so too will you when you *Stay in the Flow*.

   Close your eyes and see yourself floating along *Your Stream* toward your dream. Feel the support of the water beneath you and the energy of the universe flowing through you. Now open your eyes and describe or draw your experience.

2. Throughout the day, keep this feeling within yourself and be *In the Flow* with the universe and the world around you. Please describe how it felt to be *In the Flow* today. With your new level of awareness, you will feel your *Energetic Vibration* when you are *In the Flow*. Describe below this wonderful experience.

3. Today, did any rocks cross your path? Please describe them.

4. List the various Gifts that you used to *Stay in the Flow* or that you will use to *get back into The Flow*.

Gifts Applied

5. In the days ahead, there may be other rocks in *Your Stream*. Sometimes you can see them up ahead and can plan how you will *Stay in The Flow* when they cross your path. As you see new rocks, should they appear, please describe what they are and the choices you will make in order to *Stay in the Flow*.

Rocks   *Choices*

6. Emotions will arise as you follow your *Manifesting Dream Map*. Now that you are on your new path, you know how important it is to use the 4th Gift of *Honoring Yourself*, Recognizing Your True Self, Listening to Your True Voice, Allowing Yourself to Feel and Giving Yourself What You Need. When emotions arise, take time to *Honor Yourself* and look within. Utilize the 10th Gift of your *Detachment Muscle*. By fulfilling your needs, you will be able to *Stay in the Flow*. Write down below along with what you will give to yourself is another way of *Staying in the Flow*.

Thoughts   *Feelings*   *Giving to Myself*

7. Feelings of discouragement and fear often arise as one follows their *Manifesting Dream Map* towards their dream. If these feelings come up, know they are simply emotions. Allow yourself to feel them, Gift 4, as you stay connected to your True Self by listening to your True Voice, the source of your strength and ability to create and *Manifest Your Dream*. Should these emotions come up, you can write them below, letting them out, and then giving yourself what you need to *Stay in the Flow*, allowing it to gently take you towards your dream.

Emotions   *What I Need*

_____   _____

_____   _____

_____   _____

8. A feeling of boredom may arise on your journey. Stay aware and if you notice this emotion, decide what adjustments you can make to your *Manifesting Dream Map* that will allow you to *Stay in the Flow*. Write them below. New adjustments may be needed throughout your manifesting journey. By paying attention to your thoughts and feelings, you will be able to discover what it is you need and *Honor Yourself*, Gift 4.

_____

_____

_____

_____

9. In order to *Stay in the Flow*, it is necessary at times to make adjustments to your *Manifesting Dream Map*. You may find that something has happened externally that interferes with one of your manifesting actions. This is the time to *Stay in the Flow*. To do this, adjust your *Manifesting Dream Map*. Please write down below what rock has appeared and the adjustment that you will make so that you can flow around it and keep moving along on your *Manifesting Path. Sailing Through Life.*

The Rock   *Adjustment*

_____ _____

_____ _____

_____ _____

_____ _____

_____ _____

_____ _____

10. One of the rocks may be related to your health. Know that you have the ability to move forward, *Staying in the Flow*, during these times as well. Once you feel better, you can adjust to your new state of being. You have the ability to *Stay in Flow* regardless of what comes your way. If this rock should arise, please write above the choices that you will make to move forward on your *Manifesting Path*.

11. Sometimes when a rock appears, our False Voice can become very loud. Old false thoughts and beliefs may come up. We can become hard on ourselves. Below, please describe what your False Voice has said to you in the past. Next to each word or phrase, write what your True Voice, your voice of compassion and understanding, is saying right now. As you move forward following your *Manifesting Map*, keep Jiminy on your shoulder to remind you to be kind and supportive of yourself. Treat yourself as you would any friend who was going after an amazing dream. *Honor Yourself* and listen to your True Voice. *Stay in the Flow!*

True Voice	False Voice

12. Utilizing the 15th Gift, *Preparing for Your Personal Marathon*, will support your desire to *Stay in the Flow*. It is natural to want your dream manifested right away. Usually, though, it takes some time. When you *Traveled through Time*, you were able to *BE DO* and *HAVE* your dream. Thoughts vibrate at a very fast frequency. Physical reality vibrates at a much slower frequency. It also is comprised of time with a beginning, middle and end. Having this awareness provides you will the ability to apply this *Gift*, looking at your manifesting process as an amazing and exciting marathon versus a sprint. Patience is required. Please write a note to yourself that will support this perspective and allow you to *Stay in the Flow*.

Dear Incredible Manifestor!

13. The 18th Gift that you received on your new path, *Sustained Focus,* will support your desire and ability to *Stay in the Flow*. To utilize this gift in your manifesting adventure, you must first *Live in the NOW.* Enjoy yourself. Connect with your True Self and simply *BE* in this very moment. Right now. Feel how good you feel, how exciting it is to be in this new reality. Describe or draw what it feels like living in the *NOW.*

14. The 18th Gift of *Sustained Focus* is essential as you move forward along your *Manifesting Dream Map*. With your thoughts, emotions and behaviors in alignment, you dream is in the process of being *Actualized in the World*. Know that you are moving from one reality to another. While this is happening, you may move back and forth between the two for awhile until you are living entirely in your new reality. Understanding the process will provide you with the patience and perseverance required to Actualize Your True Self, and new reality, in the world. Know that over time, you will begin to see this new reality actualized more and more. Write below, words that your True Voice can say and actions that will support you as you move between the reality you are in now, connected with your own creative energy, and the one that you are manifesting.

Words   *Actions*

15. Living in the moment allows you to feel amazing and *In the Flow*. Knowing that you have your *Manifesting Dream Map* to follow provides peace of mind allowing you to truly know that you are moving towards your dream. You can now allow yourself to *BE In the Flow*, in this new energetic force, with the knowledge that your dream is already manifested as you DO. Please write or draw your experience of being in the world in this new way.

16. As you experience each moment, *Living Your Dream*, in the *NOW* and *BEING*, you are *Manifesting Your Dream* moment by moment. At the same time, you have your *Manifesting Dream Map* that you are following. Focusing your conscious mind, on the *HAVE* while at the same time *DOING* and *BEING*, allows you to *Stay in the Flow* moving toward the realization of your dream. Below, write specific actions that you can take, internally and externally, that will help you apply this *Gift* in your manifesting journey. Know that each time you *DO*, you are creating your *HAVE*. Enjoy your *New Way of Being in the World!*

    Within   *Without*

    _____   _____

    _____   _____

    _____   _____

17. In order to keep the frequency high, it is important to go with *The Flow*, allowing yourself to move with *the Stream of Life*. Your *Manifesting Dream Map* is a general guide to follow on your *Manifesting Path*. To *Stay in the Flow*, it is important to let go of any specific attachment to it. You now know how to adjust it as needed. Let go of any attachment to how it has to happen and allow it to happen the way it needs to.

    As you focus on your inner being, your *Energetic Vibrations*, and keeping your frequency high, you can now allow your *Dream to Manifest* in the way that it is supposed to. Relax in the knowledge that you are *In the Flow* and are *Manifesting Your Dream*, the one you visualized and experienced as you moved forward on your new path. Remember *BE, DO* and *HAVE*. On the following page, please write a note to yourself that you can read when you feel yourself becoming attached to the exact way you think it "should" happen in order to support your ability to *Stay in the Flow*.

Dear Creatively Inspired ME!

18. Recognizing what you have achieved along your *Manifesting Path* allows you to keep your *Energetic Vibration* high, and tap into the power within to continue using your *Precious Manifesting Tools* to create your dream. Below, please write which steps you have already taken as you have been following your *Manifesting Dream Map*. Notice how you feel and your inner vibration.

_____

_____

_____

_____

_____

19. When you *Partner with the Universe*, you are able to *Stay in the Flow*. You know within yourself what is meant to be will be. Please write your thoughts and feelings about destiny.

20. When you are *In the Flow*, often coincidences and synchronicities occur. As you move forward on your *Manifesting Path*, pay attention to how the universe is supporting your dream and describe these instances below.

21. There are times when, due to circumstances out of our control, what we wish to manifest does not actualize in the world. When this occurs, we can still *Stay in the Flow*. *The Flow* is the amazing energy that keeps us moving forward with a peace and ease that comes from within and from a belief that we are part of something larger than ourselves. Please write below thoughts that you have on the meaning of life and what your purpose may be during this lifetime.

CHARM NINE: SUSTAIN YOUR *Manifesting Vibration*

1. As you move forward on your *Manifesting Path*, it is essential to keep your *Manifesting Vibration* high. One way to do this is to utilize your *High Vibration Shifters*. Life ebbs and flows. Our emotions ebb and flow along with it. In order to keep your *Manifesting Vibration* high, you can use a variety of different *High Vibration Shifters*.

Create a list of actions that you can take that will increase your positive, enthusiastic *Energetic Vibration* at times when life ebbs. As you do so, consider what SHIFTS you can make through connecting with your mind and body - also with you own creativity and spirituality.

My High Vibration Shifters

★

★

★

★

★

★

★

★

★

2. There are different thoughts and emotions that *SHIFT* us into higher vibrations. *Gratitude*, your 20th Gift, is one of these. Please write down the blessings that you have received throughout your lifetime and notice how your *Energetic Vibration* rises.

3. Love also has a very high energy frequency. Below, express in words or pictures the unconditional love you have for yourself. Know that you are a unique and special person. There is only one of you. You have always been wonderful.

4. When you are connected to your True Self, you experience these emotions all of the time. Loving yourself, Honoring Yourself, giving your body, mind and spirit what is needed to keep your energy high, being grateful for YOU is all part of your 4th Gift, *Honor Yourself*. Please describe what you will do today for yourself, Gift 2.

   ★

   ★

   ★

   ★

5. As you move forward utilizing your *Manifesting Dream Map* and begin *Actualizing Your Dream in the World*, different thoughts and emotions will come up. Sometimes, though the change you are creating in your world is what you truly want with all of your heart and soul, it can be scary. If you have fearful thoughts or emotions, please write them below.

   Thoughts   *Emotions*

6. Fear of change and fear of success may come up for you as you move forward on your *Manifesting Path*. If either arise, notice the thoughts, feel the emotions and identify their source. Now write below what you discovered, the related feelings and which *Gifts* you will use to connect with your True Self and raise your *Energetic Vibration*.

Seeing	Feeling	Gifts

7. As you manifest, you are moving into a New *Way of Being in the World*. Your outer world is beginning to reflect your True Self. People may react to you in a new way. Know that you have the ability to take care of yourself. Please describe what you are seeing and feeling as your True Self is more fully *Actualized in the World*. Choose the *Gifts* that will support you in staying connected to your True Self. Write them below and indicate how you will specifically use each one.

Seeing	Feeling	Gifts

8. *Honor Yourself*, using your 4th Gift, and allow yourself to move forward on your *Manifesting Path* and towards the *Actualizing of your True Self in the World*. One of the best feelings comes from *Actualizing Your True Self in the World*. Know that you deserve it. It is your right. Give yourself the love and support that you need.

Now, write a love note to yourself. The past is the past. You did the best you could with the knowledge that you had. Believe in yourself. Know that today is the first day of the rest of your wonderful life.

Dear Amazing and Lovable ME!

_____

_____

_____

_____

_____

_____

_____

_____

8. Notice how your emotions affect the level of your *Manifesting Vibration.* Take a moment to check in with the emotions you are experiencing right now. Then, shift to an even higher vibration by using one of your *Vibration Shifters.* Continue the process as you move forward on your wonderful *Manifesting Path.*

Emotion	*Vibration Shifter*

9. Please write what your True Voice says to you when you feel that you need to follow your *Manifesting Dream Map* "perfectly" or when you find you have come across a *Rock in Your Stream.*

10. Know that you are *Experiencing the Shift* and have moved into a higher level of conscious awareness. You are choosing to be aware and to grow. Allow yourself to feel proud of the incredible person you are and the choices you are now making on your new path. Love is one of the highest vibrations. Now is a great time to utilize the 9th Gift, *Treat Others with Respect, Appreciation and Kindness* for yourself. Know that you deserve as much love and support as you give to others.

Dear Authentic ME!

11. As you move forward on your *Manifesting Map*, it is exciting to *Travel through Time* to look ahead. What do you see? If there is a particular action that you can take right now that will inspire you to reach it, please write it below. This action will raise your *Manifesting Vibration* to meet the new reality. Feel how you are *In the Flow* moving forward towards your dream. As you move forward, continue this process with the knowledge that it will support the high *Manifesting Vibration* that you are experiencing right now!

12 Write or draw, in the space below, some of the physical manifestations of your dream that are already transpiring in your new reality.

13. Moving into your new reality is so exciting. Watch as your *Manifesting Vibration* rises as the joy, from within your True Self, fills you. This joy creates a momentum that takes you forward on your *Steam of Life* towards your *Manifesting Dream*. Write or draw what it feels like as you see your dream become a reality.

The Manifesting *Oasis*

1. You have now entered the *Manifesting Oasis.* where you will have experiences that will connect you more deeply with your *Manifesting Vibration* and abilities. Within this beautiful Oasis, there are powerful energies and energetic forces. You can feel them all around you. They are in the air you breathe, the flowers and herbs that are growing all around you, the crystals, rocks and the water that flows through them and in the sky above. You can connect with this energy anytime.

    Think about what new sources of energy you will bring into your life to attract and *Manifest Your Dream*. Please write them down below.

    _____

    _____

    _____

2. This *Manifesting Oasis*, so full of life and expectancy, is contained within the *Healing Oasis*. If you discover a block or resistance that relates to past painful experiences, you can gain more information about it and then release it here. Healing the pain of the past, you will reconnect with your True Self and your amazing power to create and feel the joy and happiness that already is within you. Draw or describe any painful memory that you are feeling as you move forward on your *Manifesting Path*.

3. On your own, you can reach this *Healing Oasis* through meditation, hypnosis and sacred ceremony. Please take some time to consider how you will make this journey into new realms part of your life on a regular basis, during waking and sleeping hours, and describe them below.

4. As you learn more about your inner being from your subconscious, write your experiences and the knowledge you are gaining as you delve into these previous hidden parts of yourself.

My Reflections

LIVING IN
Passion

1. For the most part, your choices created the life that you have now, while the choices you make today will create your future. Please write all the wonderful dreams you have already made come true in your life including the dream that you have just manifested!.

2. As you continue to move forward on your new path, you will continue to Experience the Shift and Manifest new dreams. They be dreams that you have right now or dreams that you have yet to imagine. You are now Living in Passion, connected to your True Self, creating a life that truly reflects your Authentic Self in the World. Describe or draw what this feels like right now in this moment.

Congratulations on Manifesting Your Dream! Know that you deserve all the happiness that life has to offer. Allow yourself to feel and believe this with every part of your being. You have all that you need, within yourself, to create a wonderful life of passion and fulfillment.

See it! Feel it! BE DO HAVE!

Wishing you True happiness!

Bonnie Barness

My Reflections

ABOUT THE *Author*

Bonnie Barness is from Beverly Hills, California and is a graduate of U.C.L.A. She currently resides in Scottsdale, Arizona, where she maintains a private practice providing psychotherapy, hypnotherapy, and life coaching.

Ms. Barness has created a process in which individuals are able to shift out of pain, blocks, barriers, and limitations into a new state of consciousness, allowing for a greater experience of joy, happiness, fulfillment and the manifestation of dreams. This method, the Barness SHIFT Method, provides hope, relief and freedom for individuals dealing with anxiety, depression, loss and addiction. She helps couples and families move out of conflict into deep intimate connections. Those consciously on a spiritual path reach new levels of insight, understanding and experience. For some, the SHIFT takes place over a period of time. For others, it happens immediately.

As an author and speaker, Ms. Barness enjoys sharing her unique approach to life, relationships and spiritual growth with others. On radio and television, as an expert source for the Arizona Republic and in her advice column, "Ask Bonnie", she has provided specific strategies for dealing with life's challenges and for living life to its fullest.

Through her books and workbooks, *"Finding the Balance: A Guide to Sane Living"*, *"Experiencing the Shift: A Journey, to Your Authentic Self"* and *"Manifesting Your Dreams"*, as well as during SHIFT workshops and weekend retreats, she supports individual of all ages make dreams into reality. For more information about her books and events, please visit BonnieBarness.com. If you are interested in arranging future speaking engagements or a private session, please email her at Bonnie@BonnieBarness.com.

www.ingramcontent.com/pod-product-compliance
Lightning Source LLC
Chambersburg PA
CBHW061813290426
44110CB00026B/2865